Women of

Presented to:

_____

By:

_____

Date:

_____

Occasion:

_____

Women of Wisdom

Your 31-Day Devotional
for Increase and Motivation

Harrison House
Tulsa, Oklahoma

Contents

Develop Good Habits. 1

Pray in the Spirit Daily 4

Spend More Time on the Inside Than the Outside 7

Make It a Habit to Keep Things Clean and Orderly. 10

Be a Good Steward of What God Has Given You. 13

Remember to Be Thankful. 16

Dress for Success 19

Humble Yourself and Ask for Help. 22

Your Faith Will Make You Whole 25

Forgive Yourself Today. 28

Believe and Receive. 31

Expect an Uncommon Harvest 34

Write Your Vision Down 37

Make To-Do Lists 40

Be an Excellent Person. 43

Stop Looking in Life's Rearview Mirror 46

You Have Angels. 49

Never Leave Offended 52

Keep Your Word. 55

Watch Your Words 58

Be Faithful. 61

Don't Be a Complainer. 64

Stay on the Positive Side 67

Big Doors Swing on Little Hinges 70

Be a True Friend 73

Think Big 76

Faith Doesn't Pressure People 79

Confess Favor Daily 82

Remember Who You Are 85

Don't Worry; Be Happy 88

Take Care of Yourself 91

Scriptures to W.O.W. You 94

Introduction

I am so glad that the Lord somehow put this book in your hand! I don't believe it was by accident that you picked up this book, but rather the answer to my prayer for the Lord to put this book in the hands of those women who will do great things. I believe that YOU are one of those women! The fact that you are hungry for more of God proves that you are already a woman of great wisdom!

There is probably a woman, who has at one point, influenced your life greatly. I can think of a few who have touched my life along the way. One, in particular, was my second grade teacher, Ms. Offerman. She said some nice things to me, at a time that I was struggling terribly in school, and became my all time favorite teacher. Another woman, who impacted my life, was Mrs. Nelson, who was my softball coach's wife in fifth grade. She always made us feel important and told us that we were great softball players. In high school, there was also my basketball coach, who made me work hard and taught me never to say the words, "I can't". Little did I know at the time, but the Lord was using all of these women to impart wisdom to me.

One of the other women that God used to influence my life was my Aunt May. She changed my life by showing me unconditional love and was one of my favorite people while growing up. There was also Sister Loretta Mellon, a nun who preached the gospel boldly, and Shirley, who encouraged me greatly. There were also a few awesome women preachers and my pastor's wife, that God had placed in my life along the way. God has also given me a few special friends that cared about me and could make me laugh until I cried. They were also there for me literally, through "thick and thin".

All of these women have played a very special part in my life and I am thankful for each one of them. However, the number one influential "Woman of Wisdom" in my life was my mother, who I also refer to as Mom or "Mum" sometimes, because she was from Scotland. She influenced my life greatly by teaching me about the Lord. She got saved and met the Lord right before I turned 16 years old. I remember when she came home from a trip, where she gave her life to Jesus and got filled with the Holy Spirit. I could tell it was for real, and I kept her up all night asking her questions. Shortly thereafter, I gave my heart to the Lord and my life was changed forever. My Mom and I were on a quest to know God and we began to devour the Word of God and go after Him with all of our might. From that point, everything changed for good and we were never the same again.

One of my Mom's favorite scriptures was James 1:5, "If any of you lack wisdom let him ask of God, who gives generously to all without reproach, and it will be given him." She always confessed that she had great wisdom and lately I have found myself doing the same. This wisdom is available to you in the same way. God will flood your life with good when you turn to Him. It would take a whole book for me to tell you of all the wonderful things God has done. He is so good.

This book was written to give you a few practical principles in bite size pieces for each day of the month. This way you can read it quickly without feeling overwhelmed. You can also go at your own pace, or however the Lord leads you. I believe the topics in this book will help you attain a higher level of wisdom. Under each topic, there is a biblical example of its application. You will also be challenged to set goals for yourself, and at the end of each section I have included a prayer for you.

The book of Proverbs has 31 chapters, and one of the most famous women in the Bible is referred to as the Proverbs 31 woman! This woman is none other than Bathsheba. Yes, that's right, the very one who was known for blowing it big time with David, remember? However, God transformed her life and raised her up to become the example of THE virtuous woman that we all read about and want to be like! WOW! That means that you can be a great Woman of Wisdom, too!

I want to encourage you to take the 31 day challenge. If you read one chapter of this book a day, then you would finish it in about a month – give or take a few days depending on the month. You could also supplement this by reading a chapter in Proverbs each day. If you do this over and over for several months, you can expect to see an increase of wisdom and God's favor in your life. You can become that "Woman of Wisdom" as described in Proverbs 31.

Finally, I want you to know that I believe that inside of you are hidden treasures of greatness. You are capable of doing so much. I would love to hear from you after you read this book. It would mean so much to me to hear about all the great things that happen to you. You could even get an extra copy for your friends and read the book together for a month and then share all these great things with each other. I believe that you are a "Woman of Wisdom" moving toward something great today!

Your sister and your friend,
Kate McVeigh

1

Develop Good Habits

- What you do daily determines what you become permanently.

- Come apart with God, before coming apart.

- Make it a habit to pray every day. Seven days without prayer makes one weak.

- Jesus had a habit of praying and going to church. (Luke 4:16.)

- Your daily habits decide your future.

- When you are in a crisis, do you run to the phone or the throne? Get in the habit of talking to God first.

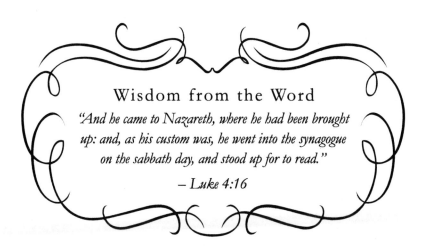

Wisdom from the Word

"And he came to Nazareth, where he had been brought up: and, as his custom was, he went into the synagogue on the sabbath day, and stood up for to read."

– Luke 4:16

A Woman of Wisdom

There is a woman in the Bible named Salome, who was the mother of James and John, two of Jesus' "inner circle" disciples. Salome was like a lot of proud mothers and wanted her sons to succeed. In fact, she was a little bit pushy! She went to Jesus and asked Him if James and John could sit at His right hand and His left hand. (Matt. 20:21.) Jesus rebuked her tenderly and turned her down, saying she didn't know what she was asking.

Now, it's easy to think of Salome's request as selfish or over ambitious. But we can't be too tough on her, since she was one of Jesus' most faithful followers and never faltered in her service to Him. She also handed down a rich spiritual legacy to her sons.

Salome obviously developed good habits in her life: habits of faithfulness to serve, habits of teaching her children and training them up in the way they should go (Prov. 22:6), and habits of spending time with Jesus and learning His ways. I'm sure she also ran her household well, or she wouldn't have had time to serve Jesus the way she did.

Your daily habits determine what you become permanently.

My W. O. W. Goal

How can I put this into my life today? _____

_____

_____

What do I expect to happen? _____

_____

_____

Challenge: Woman of Wisdom, God has great plans for you. These plans require personal deveopment on every level. I challenge you to ask the Lord what good habit you can incorporate in your life, starting today.

Let's Pray: Father, I come to You in the name of Jesus, and I thank you for my sister in Christ. She desires to develop good habits and become who You desire her to be. Give her the wisdom to know what changes need to be made and the grace she needs to succeed. I thank You for her, Father. In Jesus' name I pray. Amen.

2
Pray in the Spirit Daily

- The Bible teaches that whoever prays in tongues improves himself. (1 Corinthians 14:4 AMP.)

- Pray in tongues at least fifteen minutes every day. If you do this, then at the end of a year you will have prayed over ninety hours in tongues. Just imagine what ninety hours of prayer can do for you!

- Praying in tongues edifies you. (1 Corinthians 14:4.)

- Praying in tongues refreshes you. (Isaiah 28:11-12.)

- Praying in tongues helps your weaknesses. (Romans 8:26.)

- Praying in tongues makes you more sensitive to the Holy Spirit's leading.

- If you do not speak in tongues, ask the Lord to fill you with His Spirit.

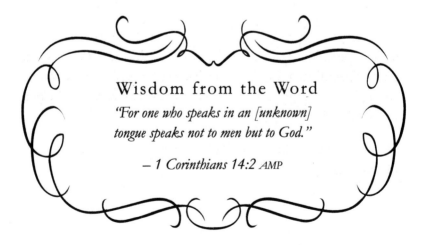

Wisdom from the Word

"For one who speaks in an [unknown] tongue speaks not to men but to God."

— 1 Corinthians 14:2 AMP

A Woman of Wisdom

O ne of the most influential women in the New Testament was Priscilla, a Jewess who came from Italy with her husband Aquila to live first in Corinth and then in Ephesus. They had churches in their homes, and she played a very important role in the early church. Paul left the work in Ephesus in the capable hands of Priscilla and her husband.

Although Priscilla had to manage her household and weave tent cloth, she found time to be a thorough student of the Gospel. She and Aquila were the ones who helped Apollos gain a better understanding of the new Christian faith as they "expounded unto him the way of God more perfectly" (Acts 18:26).

It is likely that Priscilla took the lead in these times of teaching (writers in the New Testament broke all conventionalities of the times and three times out of five placed her name before her husband's.) Christians honored Priscilla because she served God "acceptably with reverence and godly fear" (Hebrews 12:28). She was obviously an example of a woman of wisdom.

Furthermore, it is common knowledge that Priscilla prayed in the spirit, just as Paul admonished all the early believers to do (1 Corinthians 14:18). This has undoubtedly empowered, strengthened, edified and helped her in every way as she helped to lead the church.

The Bible teaches that whoever prays in tongues improves themselves.

My W. O. W. Goal

How can I put this into my life today? _____

_____

_____

What do I expect to happen? _____

_____

_____

Challenge: Woman of Wisdom, for the next thirty days, I challenge you to spend extra time in prayer– at least an extra ten minutes–praying in the Holy Spirit, and see what happens. God will reward your investment.

Let's Pray: Father, I come to You, in the name of Jesus, and pray this Woman of Wisdom will feel Your gentle nudge to invest more time praying in the Spirit. Help her see the time she has to dedicate to this challenge and make the results obvious. I thank You, Father, for this mighty Woman of Wisdom. In Jesus' name. Amen.

3

Spend More Time on the Inside Than the Outside

- What you take into your eyes and ears will come out in your hour of need.

- Spend as much time in the Word as you do putting on your makeup or doing your hair.

- Listen to the Word while getting ready in the morning. It takes some of us a long time to look good. That's a lot of Word you could be putting in your Spirit. Just think, in a year, you could be a powerhouse for God!

- Always remember, it's what's on the inside that really matters.

Wisdom from the Word

"But let it be the hidden man of the heart, in that which is not corruptible, even the ornament of a meek and quiet spirit, which is in the sight of God of great price."

— 1 Peter 3:4

A Woman of Wisdom

The Bible story of Sarah is an amazing story (Genesis 12-23). She gave birth to a son, Isaac, when she was ninety years old! She was long past her childbearing years and way too old to get pregnant, but God had promised her and her husband Abraham that they would have a child.

After God made that promise to them (when Sarah was in her late seventies), something amazing began to happen to her from the inside out. As she believed the Word of the Lord, she became more and more beautiful. We know that because Abimelech, pharaoh king over the land through which they travelled, took her into his harem, even though she was an old woman (Genesis 20).

Now think about it, kings don't usually seek to add seventy-plus year old women to their harems, which are already filled with beautiful (young) women. No, something had begun to happen to Sarah. She became radiantly beautiful from the inside out, as she began to believe God's promises.

The same can happen to you. Remember, it's what on the inside of you that really matters.

My W. O. W. Goal

How can I put this into my life today? _____

_____

_____

What do I expect to happen? _____

_____

_____

Challenge: You are a Woman of Wisdom. I challenge you to listen to some good preaching every day while you're getting ready and while you're driving in your car. If you need something good to listen to, you can download free mp3s from katemcveigh.org.

Let's Pray: Father, I come to You, in the name of Jesus, and pray for this Woman of Wisdom. Help her to see how to enhance who she is within, and cause that beauty to spill out to the world around her. Help her inner beauty shine through and make her more beautiful on the outside than ever before. Amen.

4

Make It a Habit to Keep Things Clean and Orderly

- Studies have proven that keeping things clean and orderly around you creates room for increase.

- I read about one multi-millionaire who pays someone full-time to do nothing but keep things clean around him. He says it helps him think more clearly.

- Clean those dresser drawers out, organize your closets, wash the dirty dishes, and make your bed every day. You will be amazed at the difference it will make.

- Getting the clutter out of your life will free your mind to think more clearly, and you will become more productive.

Wisdom from the Word

"For God is not a God of disorder but of peace."

– 1 Corinthians 14:33 (NIV)

A Woman of Wisdom

We all know the story of Martha and her sister Mary. One day Jesus was coming to their house for supper, and He always brought a fairly good-sized crowd with Him. You remember the story, how Martha got angry with Mary for just sitting at the feet of Jesus while she was busy in the kitchen getting everything ready (Luke 10).

Now, Martha could have used a lesson in resting at the feet of Jesus, but I don't think we should be too hard on her. I like Martha. In fact, if she lived in today's day and age, I'm pretty sure she would have had a day planner of some kind!

Martha got things done. She was a go-to kind of gal. I'll bet her kitchen was organized and spotless and you could always count on her to make things happen. Why do you think Jesus went to her house for dinner when He was in town? Martha made a habit of keeping things clean and orderly, which made her a great hostess.

Getting things organized can very often help us be more productive.

My W. O. W. Goal

How can I put this into my life today? _____

_____

_____

What do I expect to happen? _____

_____

_____

Challenge: God has given you the keys to the kingdom (that includes authority over the dishes). I challenge you to pick one room in your house that could use improvement, and make it your goal to have it cleaned and organized within the next seven days.

Even if you spend twenty minutes a day, by the end of the week you will have invested over two hours putting your life in order. If you tackle the task in tidbits, it won't seem so tiresome.

Let's Pray: Father, I come to You, in the name of Jesus, and pray you give this Woman of Wisdom the drive to meet this challenge. Help her get organized in every area that needs attention, and help her have the ability to maintain it once it's done. In Jesus' name. Amen.

5

Be a Good Steward of What God Has Given You

- Be a woman of excellence. Let your home be a reflection of Jesus.

- Keep your house clean and tidy. Be a good example.

- Maybe you are believing for a better house or car. If you will take good care of the one you have now, then God will bless you with something better.

- Take good care of what doesn't belong to you. When staying in hotels or renting vehicles, care for those things like you would your own.

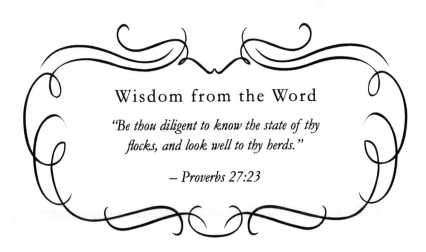

Wisdom from the Word

"Be thou diligent to know the state of thy flocks, and look well to thy herds."

– Proverbs 27:23

A Woman of Wisdom

One mother/daughter team in the Bible stands out as one of the strongest families in the New Testament, Eunice, the mother of Timothy, and Lois, his grandmother. In 2 Timothy 1:5, Paul compliments Timothy's sincere faith, giving the credit to his mother and grandmother for planting it deep in his heart.

Eunice and Lois were faithful stewards of the family and the giftings God had given them. We don't know Timothy's father's name, and it's very likely that he died when his son was a baby. That might have meant Eunice had to go out and earn a living outside her home, since the conspicuous part that grandmother Lois played could be an indication that Timothy's mother had to be away a lot.

We know from Paul's writings that Eunice and Lois passed their work ethic and their love for the Lord on to Timothy. They obviously prepared him well for the great responsibilities he undertook as a pastor in the early church. They put their hands to the daily work and childraising that was before them, and it bore great fruit. They were women of excellence.

I believe that today we are also called to be women of excellence, and let our homes, our families, and everything in our circle of influence be a reflection of Jesus.

My W. O. W. Goal

How can I put this into my life today? _____

_____

_____

What do I expect to happen? _____

_____

_____

Challenge: My challenge to you today is to take note of one area where you can be a better steward of what God has given you. Name two specific ways you can be a better steward, and then do them both.

Let's Pray: Father, I come to You, in the name of Jesus, and pray for this Woman of Wisdom. I ask You to help her see how much You've trusted her with. Give her the wisdom to know how to care for each one in a way that brings glory to You. In Jesus' name. Amen.

6

Remember to Be Thankful

- The words *thank you* can go a long way in blessing someone.

- Always send a thank-you note when someone gives you a gift. Teach your children to send thank-you notes as well. Everyone needs to be appreciated.

- Be thankful to God for the little things, as well as the big things. Thank God for the place you live, the car you drive, the friends He has blessed you with, health and strength in your body.

- Thank your parents or friends for blessing your life.

- Thank your pastor for ministering God's Word to you.

- Tell someone you appreciate them.

- Be a blessing today.

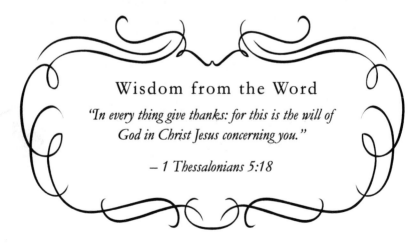

Wisdom from the Word

"In every thing give thanks: for this is the will of God in Christ Jesus concerning you."

— *1 Thessalonians 5:18*

A Woman of Wisdom

Hannah was a woman who desperately wanted a child. When we first read about her in 1 Samuel 1, she is constantly weeping and crying out to God for a baby. She is taunted mercilessly by her husband's other wife, who has children, and she suffers terribly from the shame of barrenness.

One day Eli, the priest, sees her praying and weeping in the temple, and he promises her she will have a child. As she leaves the temple, she begins to rejoice over God's promise to her, and not long after that, she becomes pregnant! Eventually she gives birth to Samuel, the priest who brings Israel back to God, and who anoints the nation's first (and second) king.

Notice that it was only when Hannah began to be thankful that her desire for a child came to pass.

Like Hannah, we have all had "barren" areas in our lives that have caused us pain. But when we praise God, He is free to shower us with His blessings. It's so important that we be thankful to God for the big things, as well as the little things.

My W. O. W. Goal

How can I put this into my life today? _____

_____

_____

What do I expect to happen? _____

_____

_____

Challenge: Today, Woman of Wisdom, I challenge you to make a conscious effort to be thankful. Spend time thanking God throughout the day, and make it a point to call or tell at least three people "thank you" for something they have done for you in your life.

Let's Pray: Father, I come to You, in the name of Jesus, and pray for this Woman of Wisdom to see all the things she can be thankful for. Open her eyes and her heart to gratitude and appreciation. From this day forward, help her to be more thankful for what You've given her. In Jesus' name. Amen.

7

Dress for Success

- Remember, you never have a second chance to make a first impression.

- It has been proven you will act the way you are dressed. If you are dressed up and looking as sharp as you can, you will act that way. However, if you are dressed sloppy, often times it will show up in your work.

- People respect you more when you are dressed properly. Make sure your clothes are ironed and your shoes are shined.

- Dress how you want to feel, not how you presently feel. Dressing nice can boost your spirit and make you feel better.

- Dress for the occasion. For example, if you are going on a job interview, make sure you dress appropriately. Often one person is chosen over another simply by how he or she dressed for the interview.

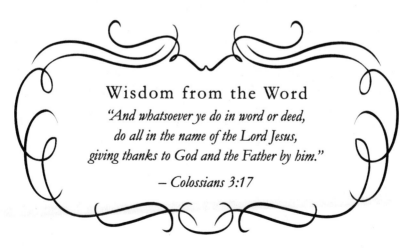

Wisdom from the Word
"And whatsoever ye do in word or deed,
do all in the name of the Lord Jesus,
giving thanks to God and the Father by him."

– Colossians 3:17

A Woman of Wisdom

The story of Esther in the Old Testament is one of beauty and courage. We first see Esther as Hadassah (her name in Hebrew), a young Jewish girl who holds no position in society. In fact, she is an orphan, who was raised in Persia by a family member, Mordecai, who works in the king's palace.

Four years later, she rises to the position of queen with a great deal of influence. Her name in Persian was Esther, which means "star." Esther went through a year of beauty treatments before she was chosen by the king as his queen, over all the other beautiful young maidens in the kingdom. (Esther 2:12,17.)

It was vital for her to become queen when she did. It was clear that she had "come into the kingdom for such a time as this" (Esther 4:14). Being chosen for her beauty and grace, put her in position to rescue her people, the Israelites, from being wiped out by the evil Haman.

Just think about taking a year to get beautiful! That's a long time, and it takes a lot of work. But Esther (and those who helped her prepare) knew the importance of looking good. Her choice to work hard at looking good helped her rise from being a Jewish orphan to being queen over all Persia.

It's important to look good. Remember, you never get a second chance to make a first impression.

My W. O. W. Goal

How can I put this into my life today? _____

_____

_____

What do I expect to happen? _____

_____

_____

Challenge: You are a Woman of Wisdom! Dress like it. Wear your best, and look your best at all times. I challenge you to make sure you look your very best before you walk out of the house every day.

Let's Pray: Father, I come to You, in the name of Jesus, and pray you help this Woman of Wisdom to look her best at all times. I pray you bless her wardrobe and her makeup kit, and give her the knowledge to use what she has to its highest potential. Help her always to represent you well. In Jesus' name. Amen.

8

Humble Yourself & Ask for Help

- If you are not a sharp dresser, find someone who is, and ask for their help.

- Ask someone to teach you how to do your hair and put on makeup. There was a time in my life when I needed help in this area, so I asked a friend to help me. (Make sure the person you are asking looks good themselves!)

- Smile.

- There are magazines you can read that will teach you proper techniques in applying your makeup.

- Don't stay the way you are just because you're too proud to ask for help. (James 4:6.)

- Do the best you can with what God has given you.

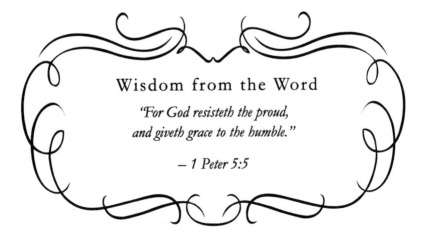

Wisdom from the Word

"For God resisteth the proud, and giveth grace to the humble."

— 1 Peter 5:5

A Woman of Wisdom

When Mary, the mother of Jesus, first became pregnant, we can only imagine how she must have felt. She was a virgin, just a teenage girl, not married, and yet she was pregnant!

She knew that she would be ridiculed by the people in her town since she was pregnant out of wedlock. She also knew that she might bring shame to her family and her fiancé, Joseph. Mary was human just like the rest of us. She probably had her share of questions and fears, even though God was clearly with her.

So Mary went to see her cousin Elizabeth, who was older, wiser, and also pregnant with John the Baptist. Elizabeth welcomed Mary and didn't ridicule her or ask questions. She knew what the Lord had done in her. They had a wonderful time together rejoicing in the Lord, the older (Elizabeth) giving comfort and advice to the younger (Mary). (Luke 1:39-56.) They ended up spending three months together.

Mary wasn't too proud to go to her cousin and get the help she needed.

My W. O. W. Goal

How can I put this into my life today? _____

_____

_____

What do I expect to happen? _____

_____

_____

Challenge: If you don't know how to do something, there's someone who does. Find them and ask them for help. I challenge you to focus on one area in your life that you can improve on, and do whatever it takes to make the investment in yourself.

Let's Pray: Father, I come to You, in the name of Jesus, and pray that you will send this Woman of Wisdom the help she needs to become all she can be. Give her the wisdom to know how to use what she learns to enhance and perfect who you created her to be and to use it to glorify You always. In Jesus' name. Amen.

9
Your Faith Will Make You Whole

- Remember the woman with the blood disease in Mark 5? Jesus said her faith made her whole.

- Your faith can make you whole in every area.

- God doesn't want you sick! Healing is His will for you—so believe it.

- The Lord once told me I could talk myself into anything. You can talk yourself right out of sickness into health, from poverty to wealth, etc.

- Call your body healed today. Confess that you are strong.

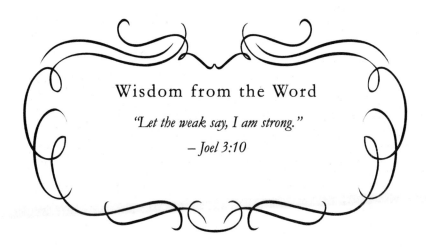

Wisdom from the Word

"Let the weak say, I am strong."

— Joel 3:10

Kate McVeigh

A Woman of Wisdom

There is a woman in Mark 5 that the Bible calls "the woman with an issue." Well, it actually refers to her as "the woman with the issue of blood." However, one day while reading this passage of Scripture in Mark, I stopped reading at the issue part and thought, *Wow, how true that is. All women have issues!*

This woman was sick. Her problem was a blood disease that she battled for twelve years. She had a major issue. She was going downhill fast. She needed a miracle and help that only God could give her.

What is your biggest issue today? Is it sickness like this woman? Is it fear? Lack of money? Problems with your children? Could it be an unforgiveness issue? One thing we know for sure, is that all women have issues. Some of us have more issues than others.

The good news is whatever your issue may be today, if you will challenge it like this woman did, it can change. I personally have overcome many issues in my own life, and I've known several women who have overcome all kinds of issues like depression, addiction, insecurity, the pain of abuse, fear, guilt, sin and the list goes on.

But God has created you to overcome and rise above your issues and conquer them. You can deal with them rather than having them deal with you. It does not matter what the issue or problem is for it cannot be bigger then God. Your issue may seem so big to you right now, but remember that many women before you have had the same problem and have overcome it.

My W. O. W. Goal

How can I put this into my life today? _____

_____

_____

What do I expect to happen? _____

_____

_____

Challenge: I challenge you, as a Woman of Wisdom, to use the faith God has given you to talk yourself to victory. Use the next twenty-one days to focus on saying what God says about every situation in your life. Refuse to say anything else.

Let's Pray: Father, I come to You, in the name of Jesus, and pray You give this Woman of Wisdom, the right thing to say at the right time. Help her see where she needs to change her conversation to line up with Your Word so she can fill those places with Your Word. I thank You, Father, for helping her. In Jesus' name. Amen.

10
Forgive Yourself Today

- Don't waste another moment living in condemnation. Forgive yourself today.

- Be like Peter, instead of Judas, and receive forgiveness. Both of these men blew it, but Peter received forgiveness. Judas did not. Peter went on to be used mightily by God, because he chose to receive forgiveness. He felt horrible about what he had done, but he got back up again. Judas, on the other hand, could not forgive himself, therefore, he committed suicide as a result.

- Let go of the past. God doesn't remember your sins when you confess them to Him. (1 John 1:9.)

- If you want to get the devil back, forgive yourself today.

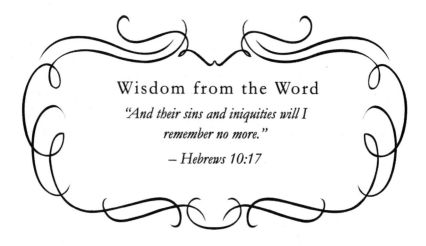

Wisdom from the Word

"And their sins and iniquities will I remember no more."

– *Hebrews 10:17*

A Woman of Wisdom

One day Jesus went to the house of a Pharisee named Simon and an unnamed woman, who was identified only as "a sinner," entered the house with an alabaster box of ointment. She washed Jesus' feet with her tears, wiped them with her hair, and kissed His feet and anointed them with the ointment (Luke 7:36-50).

Simon was shocked and basically said, "If this man (Jesus) were really a prophet, He would know who and what sort of person this woman is who is touching Him. That she is a sinner." Then Jesus told him a story of a creditor and two men who owed him money—one owed 500 pence, the other owed 50. The creditor forgave them both their debts, and Jesus asked, "Which of them will love him most?" (Luke 7:42.)

Simon answered, "I suppose that he, to whom he forgave most."(v. 43.)

Jesus told Simon that this women's sins, which were many, were forgiven, so she loved much; but to whom is forgiven little, the same loves little. (v. 47.)

Think about this woman. She was fully aware of her sin, but also fully aware of the grace and forgiveness of Jesus toward her. This shows us that there is no sin too big to forgive. He is willing to forgive all. Isn't it time we forgive ourselves and let go of our pasts?

My W. O. W. Goal

How can I put this into my life today? _____

_____

_____

What do I expect to happen? _____

_____

_____

Challenge: Woman of Wisdom, if Jesus was willing to give His life so you could be forgiven, shouldn't you forgive yourself too? I challenge you to look inside and find any unforgiveness you may be holding against yourself. If you find something–let it go–now! God can't move you forward until you move past your past.

Let's Pray: Father, I come to You in the name of Jesus, and I pray you will reveal any unforgiveness this Woman of Wisdom has against herself. Help her see how complete Your forgiveness is, and help her let it go so she can move on to the great plans you have for her. In Jesus' name. Amen.

11

Believe and Receive

- If you believe, you will receive. If you doubt, you will do without.

- Unbelief stopped the children of Israel from entering into the Promised Land. (Hebrews 3:19.)

- Many people are robbed by the thief of unbelief. Don't let doubt creep in.

- Believe His Word. Believe He will supply your needs.

- Believe He is your Great Physician.

- Believing will bring receiving into your life.

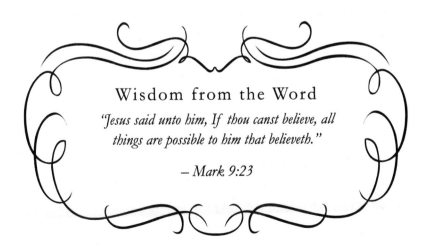

Wisdom from the Word

"Jesus said unto him, If thou canst believe, all things are possible to him that believeth."

— Mark 9:23

A Woman of Wisdom

In Luke 18, we read about a judge in a certain city who didn't fear God or respect people. And there was a widow in that city who kept coming to him and saying, "Protect and defend me, and give me justice against my enemy." (v. 3.)

For a while the judge stoutly and repeatedly refused to help her. But after she just kept persistently coming to him and asking over and over again, he said to himself, "Even though I don't fear God or respect people, because this widow continues to bother me, I will defend and protect and avenge her. Otherwise she will wear me out because she just won't give up!" (v. 4.)

Jesus used this woman as an example of the need for being persistent in our faith and our praying. He said:

And will not [our just] God defend and protect and avenge His elect (His chosen ones), who cry to Him day and night? Will He defer them and delay help on their behalf? I tell you, He will defend and protect and avenge them speedily. However, when the Son of Man comes, will He find [persistence in] faith on the earth.

Luke 18:7,8 AMP

My W. O. W. Goal

How can I put this into my life today? _____

_____

_____

What do I expect to happen? _____

_____

_____

Challenge: With God all things are possible, Woman of Wisdom. You can be, become and achieve when you believe and receive God's greatest in your life. I challenge you to stomp out doubt in your life over the next three weeks. Increase your self-talk, and focus on believing what God has told you is yours. Believe and you will receive!

Let's Pray: Father, I come to You in the name of Jesus and pray this mighty Woman of Wisdom will be stirred to stand boldly in the face of all doubt and believe Your promise no matter what. You know what she's facing, and You've made a way for her even when there seems to be no way. Give her the grace to go the distance and bring in the victory. In Jesus' name. Amen.

12
Expect an Uncommon Harvest

- God wants you to prosper so you can be a blessing. (Genesis 12.)

- You have to plant a seed if you want a harvest. And if you plant no seed, that will be your harvest.

- When you sow a seed in faith, it doesn't leave your life, just your hand. It's coming back to you multiplied.

- Lack is not God's will for you, so expect an uncommon harvest of finances to come your way.

- Call your money in by faith today!

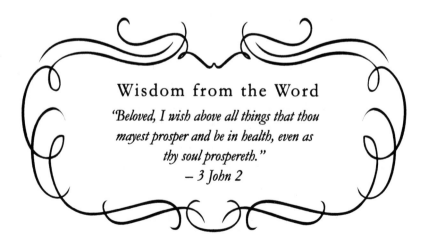

Wisdom from the Word

"Beloved, I wish above all things that thou mayest prosper and be in health, even as thy soul prospereth."
— 3 John 2

A Woman of Wisdom

The Proverbs 31 woman is an example to us all. The Bible says she diligently takes care of her household, working with her hands; she is out in the marketplace, getting the best deals and providing for her family; she gets up while it's still dark to make meals; she buys property and works the land; she prepares in advance for every season, including the cold winter, so nothing catches her or her family by surprise.

Not only that but she helps the poor and needy, she honors her husband, she is kind to everyone, and she gives wise advice. She's not lazy but diligent to see to all the things under her influence, and as a result, "Her children arise up, and call her blessed; her husband also, and he praiseth her" (v. 28).

This woman is constantly planting seed through her efforts. She is sowing in faith, and she is expecting an uncommon harvest! Because of her diligent efforts, she's never worried that her household won't be provided for.

My W. O. W. Goal

How can I put this into my life today? _____

_____

_____

What do I expect to happen? _____

_____

_____

Challenge: As a Woman of Wisdom, you are poised for increase. The Bible promises you will reap what you sow, so I challenge you to focus on opportunities to give and sow expecting an uncommon harvest.

Let's Pray: Father, I come to You in the name of Jesus and pray for this Woman of Wisdom. Open her eyes to see the many opportunities to sow kindness, time, encouragement and natural possessions. Give her the courage to be an uncommon giver who expects an uncommon harvest. I thank You, Lord, for answering this prayer and blessing this Woman of Wisdom. In Jesus' name. Amen.

13
Write Your Vision Down

- In Habakkuk 2:2, the Lord said write your vision down, so you can run with it.

- Write down the things you are believing God for as well as the things that you would like to accomplish in your life.

- One year I wrote down sixty-seven things I was believing God to do in my life. Within the first three months of writing it down, I saw over fifty of those things come to pass. Write your vision down today.

- Write down the amount of weight you want to lose, the seeds you want to sow, the business you may want to start, etc. You will begin to see amazing results after writing them down.

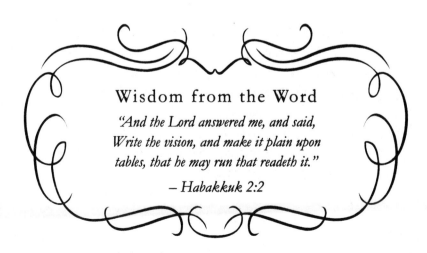

Wisdom from the Word

"And the Lord answered me, and said, Write the vision, and make it plain upon tables, that he may run that readeth it."

– Habakkuk 2:2

Kate McVeigh

A Woman of Wisdom

In the book of Joshua, after the children of Israel have conquered Jericho and other strongholds in the Promised Land, it's time for them to divide the land between the twelve tribes of Israel.

Joshua said, "Appoint three men from each tribe. I will send them out to make a survey of the land and to write a description of it, according to the inheritance of each. Then they will return to me." (Joshua 18:4 NIV.) Joshua was telling them to write a vision for the land, so they could see it in their imaginations and know how to divide it up.

Now the Bible account doesn't say that any women went along on that survey trip, but you and I know if they had, the writing might have been a little more detailed, right? Have you ever asked a man a question like, "How was the scenery?" and had them answer, "It was nice" and that's all? Sometimes men are N.I.D. (not into details), but women tend to be. I have seen amazing results when I obeyed the verse Habakkuk 2 and wrote down some of the dreams and details in my heart.

My W. O. W. Goal

How can I put this into my life today? _____

_____

_____

What do I expect to happen? _____

_____

_____

Challenge: Having direction and purpose is important for success and increase. Even if it seems like a silly desire, I challenge you to write down at least thirty dreams, goals, or desires you would like to see come to pass. Add to the list as you think of more. Save your list.

Let's Pray: Father, I come to You, in the name of Jesus, and I pray you will help this Woman of Wisdom commit her dreams and desires to paper. I trust, Lord, she will remember Your promise and this challenge when these amazing things come to pass. Amen.

14
Make To-Do Lists

- I read about a millionaire who writes down six things that he wants to accomplish every day.

- Make a to-do list. Be focused, and get something accomplished each day. Your goal should be to produce something significant every day of your life.

- When running errands or doing chores, why not map out your schedule? Write down the stores you want to go to, in order of the direction you are heading. A plan will save you time.

- Writing a to-do list unclutters your mind. It frees your mind so you can think more clearly and stay focused.

- You should own a daily planner to keep track of your appointments. Make it a new goal to be more organized.

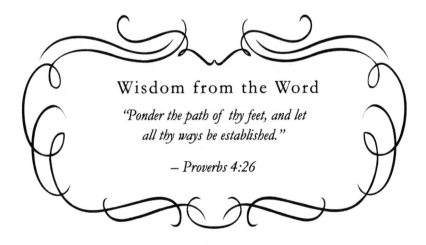

Wisdom from the Word

"Ponder the path of thy feet, and let all thy ways be established."

— *Proverbs 4:26*

A Woman of Wisdom

Dorcas was a woman who gave so generously of herself to others that even today, 2,000 years later, her name is synonymous with acts of service and charity.

She lived thirty-four miles northwest of Jerusalem at the port city of Joppa, an important center of Christianity during the years when the new faith was spreading from Jerusalem across the Mediterranean. As is often true of port cities, there were many needy people there, and Dorcas always had a heart to help them.

She also helped the widows and the orphans. Acts 9:36 NASB says she was "abounding with deeds of kindness and charity which she continually did." She didn't just give of her money, she gave of her time and herself. She was well known as a seamstress, and she, no doubt, sewed layettes for babies, made cloaks, robes, sandals and other wearing apparel for poverty-stricken widows, the sick and the aged.

Dorcas was a woman who undoubtedly had a to-do list every day! There's no way to help as many people as she did and get everything done without being organized about it.

My W. O. W. Goal

How can I put this into my life today? _____

_____

_____

What do I expect to happen? _____

_____

_____

Challenge: I challenge you to make a daily to-do list so you can use your time more wisely. Make a list of six things you want to accomplish each day, and focus your attention on getting each one done. You will feel greater satisfaction and relief as you are able to mark each completed item from your list each day. Move unfinished tasks to the next day.

Let's Pray: Father, I come to You in the name of Jesus and ask that You help this Woman of Wisdom to be more productive and focused with her time. Help her see what the most important tasks really are, and give her the grace to get them done each day. I thank You, Father, for answering this prayer. In Jesus' name. Amen.

15

Be an Excellent Person

- The Bible says that Daniel had an excellent spirit. (Daniel 6:3.)

- Do things the right way, not just the fast and easy way.

- Go the extra mile.

- An excellent person does the right thing when no one is watching.

- Do the best you can with what you have. Are you giving your all? Or are you just barely getting by?

- When I finish preaching, I ask myself three questions: *Did I do what God wanted? Did I give it my all? How could I do better?*

Wisdom from the Word

"Not slothful in business; fervent in spirit; serving the Lord."

– Romans 12:11

A Woman of Wisdom

Abigail has often been called the wisest woman in the Old Testament. She became the wife of King David after the death of her husband Nabal, who was a wealthy land owner but a drunkard. The Bible says Abigail was beautiful as well as a woman of good understanding. (1 Samuel 25:3.)

She helped to avoid a volatile situation against her household by interceding with David on behalf of her husband, who was described as "harsh and evil in his dealings" (v. 3 NASB) and had refused to give food to David and his men. David said to her, "Blessed be the Lord God of Israel, who sent you this day to meet me, and blessed be your discernment, and blessed be you, who have kept me this day from bloodshed and from avenging myself by my own hand." (vv. 32,33 NASB.)

Even though her husband didn't do things right, Abigail did things the right way.

Later, after Nabal died, David married her, and she turned out to be just the wife he needed. He was strong willed and had a temper; she was humble and gentle. She probably helped him learn patience and inspired his confidence. Abigail was a woman of excellence.

My W. O. W. Goal

How can I put this into my life today? _____

_____

_____

What do I expect to happen? _____

_____

_____

Challenge: Women of Wisdom operate in excellence. They tackle a task and always give their best effort. Today, I'm challenging you to go the extra mile. Whether it's at work or home, or in a relationship, I'm encouraging you to do everything with excellence and energy. Success in this area will catapult you to opportunity.

Let's Pray: Father, I come to You, in the name of Jesus. I'm asking you to help my sister to develop a spirit of excellence in all that she does. You have entrusted her with valuable tasks, large and small, and I pray You'll give her endurance and wisdom to see and do whatever it takes to run her race successfully. I thank You, Father, for the answer. In Jesus' name. Amen.

16

Stop Looking in Life's Rearview Mirror

- Stop looking at your past mistakes. You can't change what you did, but you can change how you are going to live life today. (Philippians 4:13.)

- If you keep looking in the rearview mirror, you may run into something. Don't park alongside your past mistakes.

- Remember, the blood of Jesus has washed your sins away.

- Your future is not based on your past.

- When the devil reminds you of your past, remind him of his future!

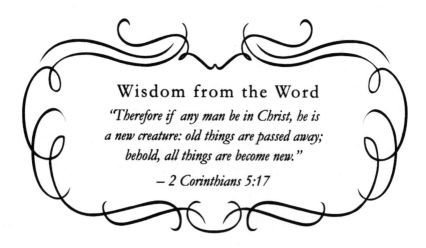

Wisdom from the Word

"Therefore if any man be in Christ, he is a new creature: old things are passed away; behold, all things are become new."

– 2 Corinthians 5:17

A Woman of Wisdom

The story of Lot's wife can teach us a lot about looking backward. Her family lived in Sodom, a city that God had determined to destroy because of its wickedness. (Genesis 13:13.)

It's easy to assume that Lot's wife was a woman who was comfortable in the evil city of Sodom. Her husband was rich and influential (Genesis 13:5,6), and she was probably a worldly, selfish woman, who spent lavishly and entertained elaborately. No doubt she was hopelessly bound up with all the evil and materialism of Sodom, worshipping false idols and committing all sorts of sin against God.

Abraham, God's covenant man, was Lot's uncle. When God told Abraham about destroying Sodom, he interceded for his nephew's family. As a result, two angels went to rescue the family before God rained fire and brimstone down on the city.

As they were fleeing the city, the angels told them, "Don't look back!" They were basically saying, "Don't look backwards and long for sin; look toward your redemption!" But you and I know what happened. Lot's wife longed for her old life. Fifteen words in the Old Testament tell her story: "But his wife looked back from behind him, and she became a pillar of salt" (Genesis 19:26).

We can learn an important lesson from Lot's wife. Don't look back at your old life, your old troubles, your old sin—Jesus has set you free from them!

My W. O. W. Goal

How can I put this into my life today? _____

_____

_____

What do I expect to happen? _____

_____

_____

Challenge: You're free to live the present and set your eyes on the future. As a Woman of Wisdom, your greatest moments lie before you. Refuse to let the past hold you back any longer. For the next two weeks, I challenge you to tell yourself every day, "I am free from the past. My faith is working for me now. My future is bright!"

Let's Pray: Father, I come to You in the name of Jesus and pray for this Woman of Wisdom to see the areas where she may be living in the past. I plead the blood of Jesus over her mind and call her "free to be" all that You have called her to be. She is free now. She is blessed now. She has a new beginning now in Jesus' name. Amen.

17
You Have Angels

- Psalm 91 says we have angels to protect us. You don't have to be afraid.

- Commission your angels to protect you and your family. Plead the blood of Jesus over your children daily.

- The angels hearken to the voice of God's Word, so speak faith-filled words today. (Psalm 103:20.)

- Speak "faith talk" which is simply talking like God talks.

- Your angels can influence people into giving you favor.

- Even though you can't see them, your angels are working on your behalf today.

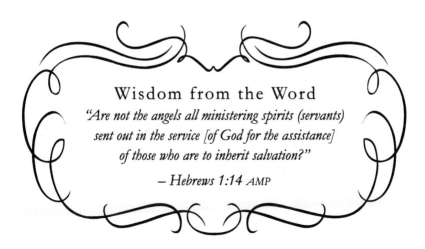

Wisdom from the Word
"Are not the angels all ministering spirits (servants)
sent out in the service [of God for the assistance]
of those who are to inherit salvation?"

– Hebrews 1:14 AMP

Kate McVeigh

A Woman of Wisdom

Hagar was a woman who was put in an unenviable position. She was a handmaiden, a servant of Sarah who was the wife of Abraham. Sarah decided that since she couldn't have any children, her handmaiden Hagar should bear Abraham a child. Hagar didn't really have any choice in the matter!

Having a baby with the maid sounds odd to us today, but in that day and age, it was a fairly common practice, especially if the master's wife was barren, as Sarah was, at that point.

The problem was, once Hagar became pregnant with Abraham's son, Hagar despised Sarah and treated her with superiority and disrespect. (Genesis 16:4.) So, as you can imagine, Sarah got angry and rebuked her, treating her so badly that Hagar fled to the wilderness.

An angel of the Lord found Hagar and told her that her son would be born, and his descendants would be multiplied. The angel also told her to go back to Sarah and submit to her authority, (v. 9.) so she did.

Angels are here to help us, just as that angel helped Hagar.

My W. O. W. Goal

How can I put this into my life today? _____

_____

_____

What do I expect to happen? _____

_____

_____

Challenge: As a child of God, you have access to His protection. As a Woman of Wisdom, you know how to walk in His protection. I challenge you to stop using words of death and doubt like, "that just kills me" or "I died laughing," and use your mouth to speak the Word in every area of life, including supernatural protection. Remember, the angels listen to God's Word and respond when it's spoken.

Let's Pray: Father, I come to You in the name of Jesus and pray for this mighty Woman of Wisdom to see any area she may be loose with her words. I pray you'll give her a greater understanding of the ministry of angels for protection and provision, and show her exactly how to use her words to be effective in the spirit realm. In Jesus' name I pray. Amen.

18
Never Leave Offended

- You should never leave a job, church or position offended.

- Don't let the devil win because someone offended you. Choose to walk in love and pray for favor in the situation.

- There is a right way and a wrong way to leave a place. Never slam doors that you may want to re-enter again at a later date. Make sure you are leaving for the right reasons.

- Remember, the grass looks greener on the other side, but it's not! There is no perfect job, church or place because people are there. Make God your total source of joy, peace and happiness.

- When someone offends you, don't nurse it, don't rehearse it. Just curse it, disperse it, and God will reverse it.

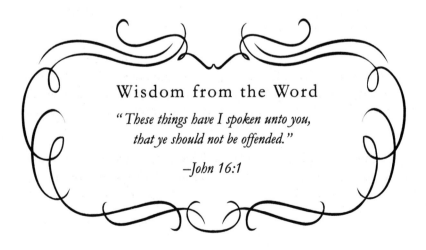

Wisdom from the Word

*"These things have I spoken unto you,
that ye should not be offended."*

—John 16:1

A Woman of Wisdom

In Mark 7, we see a woman who refused to be offended, even when she had every reason to be. The story takes place in the region of Tyre where Jesus went to visit a house and didn't want anyone to know He was there.

However, He couldn't escape notice, and after hearing where He was, a Gentile woman (of the Syrophoenician race) came to the house and fell at His feet, begging Him to heal her little daughter. The girl had an unclean spirit, and this desperate mother wanted Jesus to come and cast the demon out. You can imagine how she must have felt, begging for the deliverance of her daughter.

But Jesus said, "Let the children be satisfied first, for it is not good to take the children's bread and throw it to the dogs" (v. 27 NASB).

Think about that. Syrophoenicians were pagans, they didn't worship God, and they didn't fellowship with the Jews. Jesus basically called this woman no better than a dog! If you or I were in her position, we might have gotten offended. You could see where she might have wanted to stomp away and say, "Fine! I don't need your help if you're going to call me a dog."

But instead, the woman refused to get offended, and as a result, she received her blessing from the Lord. She persevered through the opportunity to get her feelings hurt, and instead she said to Jesus, "Yes, Lord, but even the dogs under the table feed on the children's crumbs" (v. 28).

As a result, Jesus said to her, "Because of this answer go; the demon has gone out of your daughter" (v. 29 NASB). And when she got home, she found her daughter lying on the bed, and the demon had left her.

My W. O. W. Goal

How can I put this into my life today? _____

_____

_____

What do I expect to happen? _____

_____

_____

Challenge: We all are faced with opportunities to be mad or hurt, but don't fall into the enemy's trap. As a Woman of Wisdom, the challenge I have for you today is to keep your eyes open for the opportunity to be offended and then refuse to give in. As you practice this technique, it will get easier and easier. Your future really does depend on it.

Let's Pray: Father, I come to You in the name of Jesus, and I thank You for this Woman of Wisdom. I pray You will help her see when the enemy is trying to trap her in offense. Help her take charge of her emotions and make the conscious decision to walk away from the trap so that she is always in the right place, always with the right heart, always ready to receive Your best. In Jesus' name. Amen.

19
Keep Your Word

- The Bible says we should do what we said we will do no matter what. This means we keep our word, even if it costs you.

- We reap what we sow. If we do not keep our word to people, then eventually we will find others not keeping their word to us.

- Think before you commit to something. If you're not sure you can do something, be honest. Don't put an absolute on something until you know for sure. You may have to say that you will think about it.

- My Dad always told me, "If your word is no good, you're no good." Keep your word.

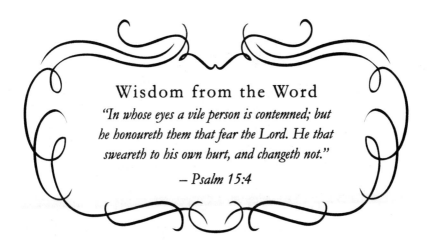

Wisdom from the Word

"In whose eyes a vile person is contemned; but he honoureth them that fear the Lord. He that sweareth to his own hurt, and changeth not."

— Psalm 15:4

A Woman of Wisdom

Rahab was a woman with a shady reputation, but the Bible says she kept her word to God's covenant people, and they kept their word to her, which resulted in her entire family being saved. She also ended up in the lineage of Christ (Matthew 1:5), and listed in the hall of fame of faith in Hebrews 11:31.

Rahab's family lived in Jericho at the time that Joshua and the children of Israel targeted it as their first conquest in the promised land. (Joshua 2:1.) Joshua sent two men in advance to spy out the land, and Rahab hid them on her roof and later helped them escape the city, even though it was dangerous for her to do so.

She made a deal with them: "Please swear to me by the Lord that since I have dealt kindly with you, that you also will deal kindly with my father's household, and give me a pledge of truth, and spare my father and my mother and my brothers and my sisters, along with all who belong to them, and deliver our lives from death." (vv. 12,13.)

The men agreed and told her to tie a red cord in her window, which would identify her house to the army of Israel, and they would harm no one in that house when they came to take the city. That's just the way it happened.

At great risk to herself and her family, Rahab kept her word to the two spies, and they kept their word to her.

My W. O. W. Goal

How can I put this into my life today? _____

_____

_____

What do I expect to happen? _____

_____

_____

Challenge: Women of Widsom can be trusted. People see them as dependable and honorable. If you say you'll do something, do it. Today I challenge you to make note of the commitments you make to other people. Are you overcommitting yourself? Do you feel like people take advantage of you? See if maybe you're causing yourself problems, and then learn to say no.

Let's Pray: Father, I come to You in the name of Jesus and ask you to help this Woman of Wisdom to be wise with her promises. Help her to know what she should commit to and then be able to keep her word. If she needs help saying no, I ask you to give her the courage to stand up without feeling guilty. Thank you, Father. In Jesus' name. Amen.

20
Watch Your Words

- Have you ever blown it by simply saying the wrong thing? I don't like it when I say the wrong thing! I have found that asking the Holy Spirit to help me guard my mouth can save me a lot of trouble. (Psalm 141:3.)

- Have you ever felt the Holy Spirit prompting you not to say something? Be sensitive and listen to Him. He could save you hours of trouble.

- My mom always told me that people who gossip *to* you, will gossip *about* you. Don't be the carrier of bad news. Maybe what you heard isn't true after all. Even if it is, that person may have repented. Besides, how would you like it if everyone knew all your mistakes?

- Think, think, think before you speak!

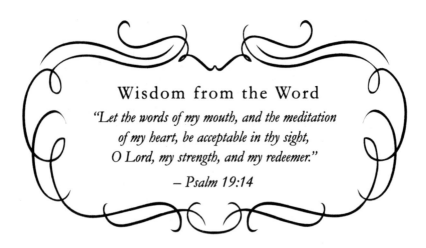

Wisdom from the Word

*"Let the words of my mouth, and the meditation
of my heart, be acceptable in thy sight,
O Lord, my strength, and my redeemer."*

– Psalm 19:14

A Woman of Wisdom

In the book of 2 Kings, we find a woman of wealth and influence in the village of Shunem, who gained permission from her husband to build a special guest room for the prophet Elisha to come and stay in whenever he was in town. (2 Kings 4:9,10.) Elisha greatly enjoyed staying there, and came often.

One day Elisha asked her how he could repay her generous hospitality, but she said nothing. However, Elisha's servant Gehazi knew that she had never been able to have children and desperately wanted to. So Elisha called her to his room and prophesied that by spring she would have a son, and she did.

Can you imagine how much she loved this boy whom she had waited so long for? I'm sure she thanked God every day for the blessing of her son.

About 10 or 12 years later, the young boy went out to the fields with his father. It was a hot day, and suddenly, out of the blue, he just cried out, "My head, my head!" (4:19) and fell over. A servant carried him home to his mother, where he lay on her lap for a while and then died.

Imagine how this mother must have felt. She didn't begin to wail or cry; she didn't speak words of doubt or unbelief. She simply took him upstairs, laid him on the bed, and went to look for Elisha, the man of God.

When Elisha saw her coming, he told Gehazi to go and ask her, "Is it well with you?" When he did, she replied, "It is well."

Now, the woman's son was dead! In the natural, it wasn't well. But she chose to speak only those words that agreed with God. She watched her words. She called those "things which be not as though they were" (Romans 4:17). When Elisha went home with her, he stretched himself out on the boy's lifeless form, and he came back to life.

What would have happened if the Shunammite woman had said the wrong thing—the doubting thing that agreed with the circumstances?

My W. O. W. Goal

How can I put this into my life today? _____

_____

_____

What do I expect to happen? _____

_____

_____

Challenge: Women love to talk, but as a Woman of Wisdom, you need to keep your conversation in line with the Word of God. If you sense the Holy Spirit telling you not to say the words that are rolling around in your head, don't! I challenge you to refrain from talking about other people in a way that would hurt or embarrass them or cause conflict if they found out what was said.

Let's Pray: Father, I come to You in the name of Jesus and pray this Woman of Wisdom will glorify You in her conversations. Holy Spirit, I ask You to cause her to know if she's about to say something she shouldn't, and help her keep her tongue in check. I thank You, Father, for answering. In the name of Jesus. Amen.

21
Be Faithful

- It's a Bible fact that the faithful person will be the blessed person. (Proverbs 28:20.)

- Sow seeds of faithfulness. Be faithful to your church, job, and friendships. God rewards faithfulness. (Hebrews 6:10.)

- When I was first saved, I served in the children's ministry at my church for several years. I was faithful to attend every service. I don't believe I would be traveling all over the world preaching today if I hadn't been faithful to serve in my home church.

- Be a faithful employee. Be honest. Be on time. Be faithful to do a good job even when no one is watching. God is watching. He will reward your faithfulness.

Wisdom from the Word
"For God is not unrighteous to forget your work and labour of love, which ye have shewed toward his name, in that ye have ministered to the saints, and do minister."
– Hebrews 6:10

Kate McVeigh

A Woman of Wisdom

The book of Ruth is a wonderful story about a young woman's faithfulness and God's reward to her for being so faithful.

Ruth was from the nation of Moab, a nation that did not worship God. She married into a Hebrew family that had moved to the land of Moab. Her husband, as well as her father-in-law and brother-in-law, all died. That left Ruth, her sister-in-law and her mother-in-law, Naomi, as widows.

Naomi gave both her daughters-in-law permission to return to their families and remain in the land of Moab, but Ruth expressed her loyalty and faithfulness to Naomi saying, "Where you go, I will go, and where you lodge, I will lodge. Your people shall be my people, and your God, my God" (Ruth 1:16 NASB). Ruth forsook her land, her heritage, her family and her old life to follow Naomi and Naomi's God.

When Ruth and Naomi returned to the land of Israel, Ruth faithfully worked in the fields to provide for herself and Naomi. She didn't ask for special attention, but the Lord was watching her faithfulness. As a result, Ruth had favor with the owner of the fields, Boaz, and she eventually became his wife.

They had a son, Obed, who gave great comfort to Naomi, and who was also an ancestor of Christ. (Matthew 1:5.) This young girl from Moab, not even part of God's covenant people, was rewarded with a loving husband, a son, and a place in the lineage of Jesus—all because of her faithfulness!

My W. O. W. Goal

How can I put this into my life today? _____

_____

_____

What do I expect to happen? _____

_____

_____

Challenge: God rewards faithfulness. To become a Woman of Wisdom, you must be faithful: faithful to God and His Word in your relationships and faithful to your church. I challenge you to spend the next week asking yourself if you're unfaithful in any way, and make the changes needed to be a good and faithful servant.

Let's Pray: Father, I come to You in the name of Jesus and pray for my sister. If there are any areas in her life where she is not faithful, shine Your light on her so she can become the Woman of Wisdom you desire for her to be. In Jesus' name. Amen.

22
Don't Be a Complainer

- I heard a great preacher say, "If you complain, you will remain."

- Never complain about what you permit. If you over schedule yourself, it's not God's fault. Quit complaining. If you don't like being overweight, stop complaining about how tight your clothes are. Do something about it.

- If you are complaining, you are not in faith. Instead of complaining about your beat-up car, start praising God for a better one. In the meantime, be thankful for what you have and expect something better.

- Don't complain and remain. Give God praise and you will be raised!

Wisdom from the Word

"Do all things without murmurings and disputings."

– Philippians 2:14

A Woman of Wisdom

Miriam was the older sister of Moses. She was part of the great Exodus as the children of Israel were delivered from bondage in Egypt. She saw many, many signs and wonders–the plagues on the land of Egpytians, God's redemption through the Passover, the parting of the Red Sea and water coming out of a rock, just to name a few.

She was courageous and a great worshipper. Yet once they were free from Egypt and travelling through the wilderness, Miriam began to have issues with her brother Moses. (Numbers 12:2.) Just like all the rest of the children of Israel, when things went wrong, she began to blame the leader (wow, this still happens today, doesn't it?).

Complaining didn't work out very well for Miriam (just like it doesn't work out very well for us). Numbers 12:9-10 says that the anger of the Lord burned against her, and she became leprous–she got leprosy all over her body.

We know that the children of Israel were kept from entering the Promised Land because of their unbelief (Hebrews 3:19) because they complained and refused to believe that God would help and deliver them. Miriam was also one of those who remained in the wilderness and never got to see the Promised Land. It's a sobering lesson that reminds us to not be a complainer.

My W. O. W. Goal

How can I put this into my life today? _____

_____

_____

What do I expect to happen? _____

_____

_____

Challenge: Who enjoys listening to a complainer? I sure don't. My challenge for you today is to zip your lips and refuse to complain no matter what happens for the next seven days. With some practice, the things that would stress you out will lose their power, and you'll find you're happier and more content.

Let's Pray: Father, I come to You in the name of Jesus. I pray You help this Woman of Wisdom take control of any negative thoughts or attitudes that are stopping her from experiencing increase or excellence in her life. Help her to see the good even in bad circumstances and to live her life with eyes fixed on You. I thank You, Father. In Jesus' name. Amen.

23

Stay on the Positive Side

- Faith always looks for the positive things. I was in a car wreck once–someone hit me from behind going 65 mph. I was not hurt, the other person wasn't hurt, and I even led the person to the Lord who hit me! I didn't focus on my wrecked car like the devil wanted me to. I looked at how God turned what the devil meant for bad into good.

- Don't focus on the negative side of life.

- If nothing really great has happened to you in a while, rejoice that nothing bad has happened. Just the fact that you're healthy, you haven't gone without food and you can see to read this book is good news.

- There is something good in every day if you look for it. Look for the positive in every situation.

Wisdom from the Word

"Rejoice in the Lord always: and again I say, Rejoice."

– Philippians 4:4

A Woman of Wisdom

In the book of Ruth, we find a woman who desperately needed to get on the positive side of life. Her name was Naomi. Naomi was Ruth's mother-in-law, and her story was indeed very sad to start with. Both Naomi's husband and her two sons died. (Ruth 1:3,5.)

We don't know what they died of, but their deaths left Naomi without support and completely grieved in heart and soul, as you can imagine. How hard it must have been to lose not only your life's partner, but two sons also. She decided to return to her family in Bethlehem, and her loyal daughter-in-law, Ruth, came with her.

God provided for Naomi in many ways in those early days of her widowhood. He brought her home safe to her family, and He made sure she had the company of her precious daughter-in-law to take care of her. He supernaturally gave Ruth favor in the fields so they had plenty to eat. However, Naomi was only focused on the pain, the loss, the grief.

When she greeted her family members, she said, "Do not call me Naomi; call me Mara (which means "bitter"), for the Almighty has dealt very bitterly with me. I went out full, but the Lord has brought me back empty. Why do you call me Naomi, since the Lord has witnessed against me and the Almighty has afflicted me?" (Ruth 1:20,21).

While it's easy to understand the source of Naomi's pain, it's so important to remember that faith stays on the positive side, and in agreement with God and His promises. It's easy to get depressed over circumstances, but that doesn't help the situation.

My W. O. W. Goal

How can I put this into my life today? _____

_____

_____

What do I expect to happen? _____

_____

_____

Challenge: Staying positive in a negative world can be a challenge, but as a Woman of Wisdom, you're more than able. God's Word will help you stay anchored in His grace and a heart of praise will keep you focused in the right direction. My challenge to you is to make yourself say something positive every time something looks or feels negative.

Let's Pray: Father, I come to You, in the name of Jesus, and pray that Your amazing grace will help this Woman of Wisdom to stay focused on the positive promises and encouragement in Your Word regardless of what's going on in her world. Help her stay on track and keep moving toward becoming all she is in Christ. In Jesus' name. Amen.

24

Big Doors Swing on Little Hinges

- Little things add up. Eating a "little" candy bar here and a "little" ice cream there makes all the difference in the world.

- Don't despise small opportunities. I've preached in some little places that have led to the most incredible opportunities.

- Don't belittle your position. If you're in the ministry of helps, do an excellent job. You may feel like what you're doing is little, but remember that the mighty oak tree started as a little acorn.

- Give someone a little encouragement today. It's the little cards and words of encouragement that can make all the difference in someone's life.

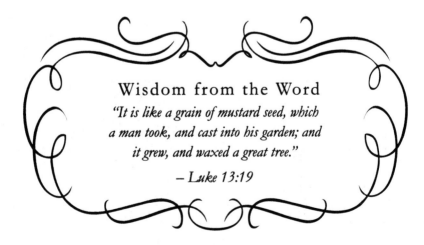

Wisdom from the Word

"It is like a grain of mustard seed, which a man took, and cast into his garden; and it grew, and waxed a great tree."

– Luke 13:19

A Woman of Wisdom

I once heard someone say "big doors swing on little hinges." I like that! It means that little things matter. And little things can become big things.

We see a woman in Mark 12, who understood that her "little thing," wasn't to be despised. She brought two small coins to the temple as an offering, and Jesus saw her. In fact, the Bible says He was sitting down opposite the offering bucket, checking out what people gave. (v. 41.) (Wouldn't that surprise some people in church today if the pastor sat down and watched what everyone put in?)

The Bible says, "A poor widow came and put in two small copper coins, which amount to a cent. Calling His disciples to Him, Jesus said to them, 'Truly I say to you, this poor widow put in more than all the contributors to the treasury; for they all put in out of their surplus, but she, out of her poverty, put in all she owned, all she had to live on'" (vv. 42-44 NASB).

Jesus praised this little woman's gift, even though it looked small to the disciples. You could say she gave her two-cents' worth! And Jesus used her as an example.

What gift do you have? Maybe you thought it was too little to matter, or that it was "less than" what someone else had to offer.

My W. O. W. Goal

How can I put this into my life today? _____

_____

_____

What do I expect to happen? _____

_____

_____

Challenge: God has big opportunities planned for you, but it's the smaller ones that determine if you ever make it to the bigger ones. A Woman of Wisdom will prosper in all she puts her hand to because she always strives to be her best and give her best. I challenge you to spend the next week thanking God for the opportunities you have right now to show forth His glory through your life.

Let's Pray: Father, I come to You in the name of Jesus and pray You send this Woman of Wisdom many opportunities to be a blessing today. Help her have the right attitude and the words that are needed to encourage someone else. Help her find great joy in being Your hand extended to a hurting world. In Jesus' name. Amen.

25

Be a True Friend

- If you want more friends, be friendly. Sow friendship so you can reap friendship. (Proverbs 18:24.)

- Learn to encourage your friends. Be a good listener. Some of my closest friends don't preach at me all the time. They listen, and they care, which means a lot to me.

- Be honest with your friends. I was trying on clothes at the mall one time and asked a friend how it made me look. She said it made me look like a cow! We laughed, and I was glad she was honest. A real friend will tell you the truth.

- Don't repeat things your friends tell you in confidence. Repeating secrets separates friends. (Proverbs 16:28.)

Wisdom from the Word

"A friend loveth at all times."

— *Proverbs 17:17*

A Woman of Wisdom

In the Bible, a woman named Elizabeth holds two distinctions that make her notable. First, she was the mother of John the Baptist. Second, she was the cousin and friend of Mary, the mother of Jesus.

We know that Elizabeth was a godly woman. She was not only the wife of a priest, but the daughter in a family of priests. Luke 1:6 NASB says that Elizabeth and her husband "were both righteous in the sight of God, walking blamelessly in all the commandments and requirements of the Lord."

Elizabeth was well past her childbearing years when God performed a miracle and she became pregnant with John. When she was about six months pregnant, her young cousin, Mary, became pregnant with Jesus and came to see her. Mary had a lot on her plate at that time, being a young teenager virgin, who was pregnant.

Have you ever had things going on in your life and needed a really good friend to help you through it? That's what Elizabeth was to Mary. She didn't turn Mary away saying, "Listen, I'm pregnant, too, and I don't have time or energy to take care of you!"

No, in her unselfish way, Elizabeth was a true friend to Mary. Mary ended up staying with her for three months, and during that time, they no doubt unburdened their hearts to each other, joyfully planning for the births of their sons, who would be so close in age.

It's important to have good friends and to be a good friend. A true friend listens and encourages.

My W. O. W. Goal

How can I put this into my life today? _____

_____

_____

What do I expect to happen? _____

_____

_____

Challenge: Being a good friend means knowing when to talk and when to listen. It means being trustworthy and dependable. I challenge you today to measure the quality of your friendships. Is there anything you can do to be a better friend? Can you be more encouraging? Listen more? Find something you can do, and then become the best friend you can be.

Let's Pray: Father, I come to You in the name of Jesus and pray for this special woman's friendships. Help her connect with godly friends and develop friendships that last—healthy, solid, friendships that enhance who You have created her to be. Help this Woman of Wisdom become a good friend just like You. In Jesus' name. Amen.

26
Think Big

- Your life will go in the direction of your most dominant thoughts. Proverbs 23:7 tells us that we are what we think.

- See yourself prospering. If you can conceive it, you can receive it. Some people say, "I could never imagine myself doing that!" That is why they are not.

- Scientists have proven that the bumblebee cannot fly. They say that its wings are too small and its body too big. But guess what? A bumblebee believes he can fly, so he does.

- Ephesians 3:20 says that God is able to do exceedingly, abundantly above all we ask or THINK! So dream big, think big and believe big–and you will receive big.

Wisdom from the Word

"For as he thinketh in his heart, so is he."

– Proverbs 23:7

A Woman of Wisdom

The only woman in the Bible, who was placed at the height of political power in Israel, was Deborah. She was a prophetess and a judge. (Judges 4:4.) There are only a few women in history who have ever attained the public dignity and authority that she did.

In the day and age in which Deborah lived, judges not only judged people and their issues, but they were chiefs and heroes as well, and their influence was mainly felt in war. As a counselor in time of peace, Deborah became known, far and wide, for her wisdom, especially in times of war.

When the people of Israel cowered in fear because of their enemies, Deborah boldly took action. She thought big! She believed that God would help them win a mighty victory. She approached Barak, the general of the army, and said, "Behold, the Lord, the God of Israel, has commanded, 'Go and march to Mount Tabor, and take with you ten thousand men from the sons of Naphtali and from the sons of Zebulun.

'I will draw out to you Sisera, the commander of Jabin's army, with his chariots and his many troops to the river Kishon, and I will give him into your hand'" (vv. 6,7).

Barak saw her spiritual insight and her boldness and said, "If you'll go with me, then I will go; but if you will not go with me, I will not go" (v. 8).

Wow! That's one of the most unusual passages ever spoken by a man, to a woman, in the Bible. But Deborah was a woman who had faith in God, and refused to fear. She only entertained thoughts of victory, and her faith was contagious.

My W. O. W. Goal

How can I put this into my life today? _____

_____

_____

What do I expect to happen? _____

_____

_____

Challenge: If you are going to grow and go where God has planned, you're going to have to think BIG, Sister! Today I'm challenging you to take note of any self-talk that would discount or discredit the dream God has placed in your heart. If you catch some doubt running about, kick it out! Stop selling yourself short. If you agree with God, you're going to get where He wants you to be.

Let's Pray: Father, I come to You in the name of Jesus and pray You will help this Woman of God take the cap off her thinking and dream Your dreams. Help her to think BIG; to see BIG; to become all that You desire. Help her to be an example to others that with God all things are possible. In Jesus' name. Amen.

27

Faith Doesn't Pressure People

- We must learn to trust totally in God to meet our needs. When you know that God is your source, you won't put pressure on people.

- Getting in faith will take the pressure off you to make things happen. Pray and ask God to speak to people on your behalf. Your angels can influence people to buy from your business. Trust God - it's a lot more exciting.

- Don't let people pressure you into doing something you don't feel led to do, and don't put pressure on other people.

- Make God your total source!

Wisdom from the Word

"Trust in the Lord with all thine heart;
and lean not unto thine own understanding."

— Proverbs 3:5

A Woman of Wisdom

After the prophet Elijah told evil King Ahab that it wouldn't rain for years, God told Elijah to go hide at the brook Cherith, and there ravens would provide for him. (1 Kings 17.)

Eventually the brook dried up, and God told Elijah, "Arise, go to Zarephath, which belongs to Sidon, and stay there; behold, I have commanded a widow there to provide for you" (v. 9 NASB).

Now, of all the people in the town, God sent him to a poor little widow. This didn't seem to make much sense, but God had a plan in mind, and part of that plan was to bless the widow.

When Elijah arrived at her house, she was preparing a meal for herself and her son. Apparently it was going to be their last meal, because she was out of food. Elijah asked her to fix him some, and she answered, "I have no bread, only a handful of flour in the bowl and a little oil in the jar; and behold, I am gathering a few sticks that I may go in and prepare for me and my son, that we may eat it and die" (v. 12).

Things were looking really bad for her! Elijah said "For this is what the LORD, the God of Israel says." 'The bowl of flour shall not be exhausted, nor shall the jar of oil be empty, until the day that the Lord sends rain on the face of the earth.'" So she went and did according to the word of Elijah, and it happened just the way God had said, and her household ate for many days. The bowl of flour and the jar of oil never ran out.

You see, God always has a way to provide. You can trust Him and make Him your total source.

My W. O. W. Goal

How can I put this into my life today? _____

_____

_____

What do I expect to happen? _____

_____

_____

Challenge: A Woman of Wisdom knows who her source is. You don't have to pressure people to be or do something for you. You have God. Today I challenge you to keep your eyes on Him and not look to someone else to meet your spiritual, emotional, physical or natural needs. He loves you!

Let's Pray: Father, I come to You in the name of Jesus and ask You to help this mighty Woman of Wisdom to keep her eyes on You. You are the Source of all she needs, and You have provided every answer. Give her a deeper revelation of how much You love her and manifest Yourself to her in obvious ways. In Jesus' name. Amen.

28
Confess Favor Daily

- A minister-friend of mine says, "One day of favor is worth a thousand days of labor."

- Think about this: favor caused Joseph to go from the pit to the palace in twenty-four hours.

- Confess and believe for favor daily. The results are amazing. You will find deals on clothes, food and even get a good parking spot when you believe for favor.

- Pray that your children will have favor with their teachers, coaches and friends.

- Pray that you and your husband (if you're married), will have favor at work. Say it daily. It works!

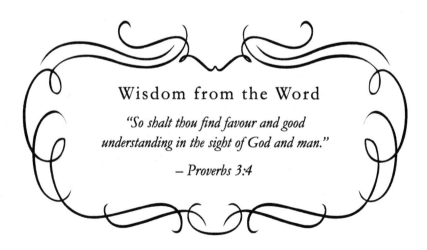

Wisdom from the Word

"So shalt thou find favour and good understanding in the sight of God and man."

– Proverbs 3:4

A Woman of Wisdom

The story of Esther is a story of great favor. Esther was just a young girl when she and all the other young women of the kingdom were called upon to participate in a country-wide beauty contest where the winner would be chosen queen.

The Bible says, "Esther was taken to the king's palace into the custody of Hegai, who was in charge of the women. Now the young lady pleased him and found favor with him, so he quickly provided her with cosmetics and food, gave her seven choice maids from the king's palace and transferred her and her maids to the best place in the harem. (Esther 2:8,9.)

In the end, it was Esther who caught the king's eye, and he chose her as queen over all the other beautiful women in the contest.

Esther didn't do anything to deserve the favor of Hegai. She just received his favor. And it helped promote her to the top of the heap! Favor can do the same thing for you. Psalm 5:12 says that God will surround you with favor as with a shield.

My W. O. W. Goal

How can I put this into my life today? _____

_____

_____

What do I expect to happen? _____

_____

_____

Challenge: As a Woman of Wisdom, you need God's favor operating in your life. I challenge you to ask God to send His favor before you every day for the next two weeks, and see what happens. I believe doors of opportunity will open, you will meet special people, good things will happen and you'll have such an exciting adventure you won't want to stop believing for it!

Let's Pray: Father, I come to You in the name of Jesus, and I pray Your favor goes before this Woman of Wisdom. Your favor shield protects her and goes before her, clearing a path and making a way where there is no way. Thank You, Lord, for Your goodness and Your favor. In Jesus' name. Amen.

29

Remember Who You Are

- Don't allow the devil or other people to intimidate you. The Greater One lives inside you! You have God's nature, ability and life in you.

- You are special, important and valuable. Your heavenly Father made you unique.

- Your position is important to God.

- Be the best you can be where God has you now.

- Your worth and value is not in what you do, but who you are in Him. Hold your head up high today and remember who lives inside you—the mighty Holy Spirit!

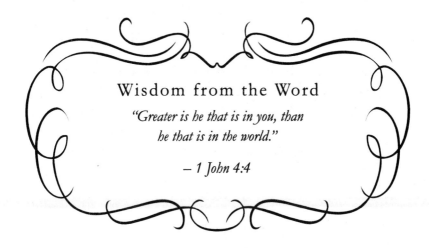

Wisdom from the Word

"Greater is he that is in you, than he that is in the world."

— 1 John 4:4

A Woman of Wisdom

In Judges 9, Abimelech was the ruler over Israel, and the Bible says there was an evil spirit between him and the men of Shechem. (v. 23.) As the battle raged between these two enemies, Abimelech ended up dying–in a very unusual way.

He and his men were getting ready to attack a tower in the city where many of the leaders of the city had gone to hide because it was a safe place.

As Abimelech approached the door of the tower, prepared to set it on fire and kill all those inside, the Bible says, "A certain woman threw an upper millstone on Abimelech's head, crushing his skull. Then he called quickly to the young man, his armor bearer, and said to him, 'Draw your sword and kill me, so that it will not be said of me, "A woman slew him."' So the young man pierced him through, and he died" (vv. 53,54 NASB).

It's not very often in Scripture that we see a woman kill a great leader. But this was apparently a gutsy woman who would do anything to protect herself and those with her. I like this lady!

First of all, she was in the tower–just like you and I are hidden in the safety of God's tower. Second, she dropped the rock on her enemy's head, just like you and I drop the Word of God on our enemy's head.

My W. O. W. Goal

How can I put this into my life today? _____

_____

_____

What do I expect to happen? _____

_____

_____

Challenge: A Woman of Wisdom realizes who she is in Christ. Without this knowledge, you will let people continue to walk on you or take advantage of you. Don't let the devil do it to you anymore. I challenge you to meditate on the Scriptures at the back of this book and become the new creation God says you are in Christ. With this understanding, he won't be able to pull the wool over your eyes anymore.

Let's Pray: Father, I come to You in the name of Jesus and pray you will help this Woman of Wisdom to see who she is in Christ. Help her learn to use her authority and the other principles we've learned to stand against the devil and claim the promises that belong to her through You. In Jesus' name. Amen.

30

Don't Worry; Be Happy

- Cast your cares on God today. Give your worries and cares to Him, and believe He will work them out. He will because He cares for you.

- Philippians 4:6 tells us that we are not to worry about anything! That means you shouldn't worry about your kids, money, people or anything else.

- Think about what you're thinking about. Don't allow your mind to think on anything it wants to. Keep your mind on the Word and what God says about your problem, and then you will have peace.

Wisdom from the Word

"Thou wilt keep him in perfect peace,
whose mind is stayed on thee:
because he trusteth in thee."

—Isaiah 26:3

A Woman of Wisdom

There is a widow in 2 Kings 4 who was in terrible trouble. Not only had her husband died, but he'd left her in debt, and the creditors were coming after her.

Now, they weren't just coming to take her house away. They were coming to take her sons away and make them slaves! Can you imagine how horrible that would be? I don't think any of us has ever been in that much trouble.

So the woman sought help from the prophet Elisha, and he asked her, "What do you have in the house?" And she said, "I don't have anything except a jar of oil" (v. 2 NASB). Elisha told her to go and borrow as many pots, pans, jars and containers as possible from her neighbors.

Once she had, he told her to "shut the door behind you and your sons, and pour out into all these vessels, and you shall set aside what is full." So she did it—and kept pouring until every container was full! It was a miracle.

Then Elisha told her to sell the oil and pay off her debt and then she and her sons could live on the rest.

My W. O. W. Goal

How can I put this into my life today? _____

_____

_____

What do I expect to happen? _____

_____

_____

Challenge: A Woman of Wisdom doesn't let worry consume her. I challenge you to shut off fear and worry and let God be God in your life. For the next seven days, refuse to worry. Any time fear or worry tries to creep in, start praising God wholeheartedly. When you magnify Him, your problems will shrink.

Let's Pray: Father, I come to You in the name of Jesus and thank You for this Woman of Wisdom. She is a mighty woman of God, and I bind worry and fear in her life. I plead the blood of Jesus over her mind and proclaim she is free from worry. She is free from fear. Give her the courage to stand boldly in the face of any situation and praise You. In Jesus' name. Amen.

31

Take Care of Yourself

- You only have one body. First Corinthians 6:19 says your body is the temple of the Holy Spirit. Take care of it!

- Get enough sleep. You'll think better, act sweeter and enjoy life a lot more if you're well rested.

- Do some kind of exercise. In my own life, I notice a big difference in my energy level when I exercise. I feel so much better. I believe you will too.

- Don't over-schedule yourself. You can only do so much, and you are only one person.

- Never make important decisions when you are tired. You don't think as clearly. God wants us to work, but He also wants us to enjoy our lives.

- God, Himself, even took a day to rest after creating the world.

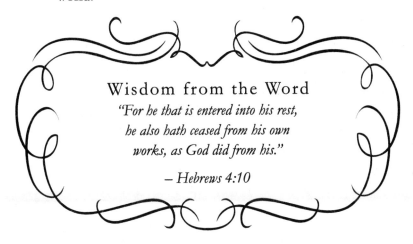

Wisdom from the Word
"For he that is entered into his rest,
he also hath ceased from his own
works, as God did from his."

– Hebrews 4:10

A Woman of Wisdom

W e've already talked about Dorcas and what a dedicated woman of service she was. She did so many good works, and she was a blessing to many who needed her.

However, what we didn't mention before was that she died suddenly. The Bible says, "She fell sick and died" (Acts 9:37 NASB). We don't know for sure, but I believe Dorcas died young from not taking care of herself. She worked so hard, that it weakened her body to the point of death, or to the point of not being able to resist sickness or disease.

Now, thankfully, Peter was able to come and raise Dorcas from the dead. (vv. 40,41.) So the story ends in victory, praise the Lord!

But I think it's something we need to take note of and implement in our lives. It is possible to work too hard in service to the Lord, not taking time to rest and refresh yourself. If you don't take care of yourself, no one else will. And you are more use to the kingdom of God if you are healthy, well-rested and living a life of balance.

I believe Jesus wants us to rest and refresh ourselves. In Matthew 11:28 AMP He said, "Come to Me, all you who labor and are heavy-laden and overburdened, and I will cause you to rest. [I will ease and relieve and refresh your souls]."

My W. O. W. Goal

How can I put this into my life today? _____

_____

_____

What do I expect to happen? _____

_____

_____

Challenge: A Woman of Wisdom honors God through moderation and good stewardship. If you don't take care of the body He has given you, it may give out too soon. I challenge you to look at what you're doing and see what changes need to be made. Are you getting enough sleep? What are you eating? Do you need to exercise? If there's an area in which you're lacking, do something about it.

Let's Pray: Father, I come to You in the name of Jesus, and I pray you will give this Woman of Wisdom a plan for taking care of her spirit, soul and body so she can run her whole race without sickness or disease. Help her find time to exercise and get enough rest. Help her see the value in taking care of what You've given her. In Jesus' name I pray. Amen.

Scriptures to W. O. W. You

And he came to Nazareth, where he had been brought up: and, as his custom was, he went into the synagogue on the sabbath day, and stood up for to read. – *Luke 4:16*

For one who speaks in an [unknown] tongue speaks not to men but to God. – *1 Corinthians 14:2 AMP*

But let it be the hidden man of the heart, in that which is not corruptible, even the ornament of a meek and quiet spirit, which is in the sight of God of great price. – *1 Peter 3:4*

For God is not a God of disorder but of peace. –*1 Corinthians 14:33 NIV*

Be thou diligent to know the state of thy flocks, and look well to thy herds. – *Proverbs 27:23*

In every thing give thanks; for this is the will of God in Christ Jesus concerning you. – *1 Thessalonians 5:18*

And whatsoever ye do in word or deed, do all in the name of the Lord Jesus, giving thanks to God and the Father by him. – *Colossians 3:17*

For God resisteth the proud, and giveth grace to the humble. – *1 Peter 5:5*

Let the weak say, I am strong. – *Joel 3:10*

And their sins and iniquities will I remember no more.
– *Hebrews 10:17*

Jesus said unto him, If thou canst believe, all things are possible to him that believeth. – *Mark 9:23*

Beloved, I wish above all things that thou mayest prosper and be in health, even as thy soul prospereth. – *3 John 2*

And the Lord answered me, and said, Write the vision, and make it plain upon tables, that he may run that readeth it. – *Habakkuk 2:2*

Ponder the path of thy feet, and let all thy ways be established. – *Proverbs 4:26*

Not slothful in business; fervent in spirit; serving the Lord. – *Romans 12:11*

Therefore if any man be in Christ, he is a new creature: old things are passed away; behold, all things are become new. – *2 Corinthians 5:17*

Are not the angels all ministering spirits (servants) sent out in the service [of God for the assistance] of those who are to inherit salvation? – *Hebrews 1:14* AMP

These things have I spoken unto you, that ye should not be offended. –*John 16:1*

In whose eyes a vile person is contemned; but he honoureth them that fear the Lord. He that sweareth to his own hurt, and changeth not. – *Psalm 15:4*

Let the words of my mouth, and the meditation of my heart, be acceptable in thy sight, O Lord, my strength, and my redeemer. — *Psalm 19:14*

For God is not unrighteous to forget your work and labour of love, which ye have shewed toward his name, in that ye have ministered to the saints, and do minister. — *Hebrews 6:10*

Do all things without murmurings and disputings. — *Philippians 2:14*

Rejoice in the Lord always: and again I say, Rejoice. — *Philippians 4:4*

It is like a grain of mustard seed, which a man took, and cast into his garden; and it grew, and waxed a great tree. — *Luke 13:19*

A friend loveth at all times. — *Proverbs 17:17*

For as he thinketh in his heart, so is he. — *Proverbs 23:7*

Trust in the Lord with all thine heart; and lean not unto thine own understanding. — *Proverbs 3:5*

So shalt thou find favour and good understanding in the sight of God and man. — *Proverbs 3:4*

Greater is he that is in you, than he that is in the world. — *1 John 4:4*

Thou wilt keep him in perfect peace, whose mind is stayed on thee: because he trusteth in thee. — *Isaiah 26:3*

For he that is entered into his rest, he also hath ceased from his own works, as God did from his. — *Hebrews 4:10*

Proverbs 31 NKJV

¹ *The words of King Lemuel, the utterance which his*
  mother taught him:

² *What, my son?*

  And what, son of my womb?

  And what, son of my vows?

³ *Do not give your strength to women,*

  Nor your ways to that which destroys kings.

⁴ *It is not for kings, O Lemuel,*

  It is not for kings to drink wine,

  Nor for princes intoxicating drink;

⁵ *Lest they drink and forget the law,*

  And pervert the justice of all the afflicted.

⁶ *Give strong drink to him who is perishing,*

  And wine to those who are bitter of heart.

  And remember his misery no more.

⁸ *Open your mouth for the speechless,*

  In the cause of all who are appointed to die.

⁹ *Open your mouth, judge righteously,*

  And plead the cause of the poor and needy.

¹⁰ *Who can find a virtuous wife?*

  For her worth is far above rubies.

¹¹ *The heart of her husband safely trusts her;*

  So he will have no lack of gain.

¹² *She does him good and not evil*

   All the days of her life.

¹³ *She seeks wool and flax,*

   And willingly works with her hands.

¹⁴ *She is like the merchant ships,*

   She brings her food from afar.

¹⁵ *She also rises while it is yet night,*

   And provides food for her household,

   And a portion for her maidservants.

¹⁶ *She considers a field and buys it;*

   From her profits she plants a vineyard.

¹⁷ *She girds herself with strength,*

   And strengthens her arms.

¹⁸ *She perceives that her merchandise is good,*

   And her lamp does not go out by night.

¹⁹ *She stretches out her hands to the distaff,*

   And her hand holds the spindle.

²⁰ *She extends her hand to the poor,*

   Yes, she reaches out her hands to the needy.

²¹ *She is not afraid of snow for her household,*

   For all her household is clothed with scarlet.

²² *She makes tapestry for herself;*

   Her clothing is fine linen and purple.

²³ *Her husband is known in the gates,*

   When he sits among the elders of the land.

²⁴ She makes linen garments and sells them,

    And supplies sashes for the merchants.

²⁵ Strength and honor are her clothing;

    She shall rejoice in time to come.

²⁶ She opens her mouth with wisdom,

    And on her tongue is the law of kindness.

²⁷ She watches over the ways of her household,

    And does not eat the bread of idleness.

²⁸ Her children rise up and call her blessed;

    Her husband also, and he praises her:

²⁹ "Many daughters have done well,

    But you excel them all."

³⁰ Charm is deceitful and beauty is passing,

    But a woman who fears the LORD, she shall be praised.

³¹ Give her of the fruit of her hands,

    And let her own works praise her in the gates.

PRAYER OF SALVATION

God loves you—no matter who you are, no matter what your past. God loves you so much that He gave His one and only begotten Son for you. The Bible tells us that "...whoever believes in him shall not perish but have eternal life" (John 3:16 NIV). Jesus laid down His life and rose again so that we could spend eternity with Him in heaven and experience His absolute best on earth. If you would like to receive Jesus into your life, say the following prayer out loud and mean it from your heart.

Heavenly Father, I come to You admitting that I am a sinner. Right now, I choose to turn away from sin, and I ask You to cleanse me of all unrighteousness. I believe that Your Son, Jesus, died on the cross to take away my sins. I also believe that He rose again from the dead so that I might be forgiven of my sins and made righteous through faith in Him. I call upon the name of Jesus Christ to be the Savior and Lord of my life. Jesus, I choose to follow You and ask that You fill me with the power of the Holy Spirit. I declare that right now I am a child of God. I am free from sin and full of the righteousness of God. I am saved in Jesus' name. Amen.

If you prayed this prayer to receive Jesus Christ as your Savior for the first time, please contact us on the Web at **www.harrisonhouse.com** to receive a free book.

Or you may write to us at

Harrison House • P.O. Box 35035 • Tulsa, Oklahoma 74153

About the Author

K ate McVeigh is in tremendous demand as one of the most sought after women speakers in America today. Kate is known as an encouraging, practical and solid Bible teacher. As an evangelist, she travels extensively speaking in churches and conferences encouraging people from all walks of life, generations and denominations, motivating and teaching them how to receive God's best.

Kate's ministry reaches thousands every day through her daily radio broadcast *The Voice of Faith* as well as her weekly television broadcast. Kate is a noted author of several books including her best-sellers *The Blessing of Favor* and *Get Over It*. Kate's message of encouragement, favor and God's love has influenced multitudes around the world into becoming all God has called them to be!

If you wish to contact Kate McVeigh:

Kate McVeigh Ministries
PO Box 1688
Warren, MI 48090
(586)795-8885

Or visit on the web at:
www.katemcveigh.org

The Harrison House Vision

Proclaiming the truth and the power

Of the Gospel of Jesus Christ

With excellence;

Challenging Christians to

Live victoriously,

Grow spiritually,

Know God intimately.